The first four presidents of the University, in academic robes, 1918: (left to right) William Watts Folwell, Cyrus Northrop, George Vincent, and Marion Burton.

Best Wishes! Prof-T.

Congratulations! Dave Odde

University Band cymbalist, 1977.

THE UNIVERSITY LIBRARY

AND THE AUTHOR

GRATEFULLY ACKNOWLEDGE

THE SUPPORT OF THE

UNIVERSITY FOUNDATION

IN PUBLISHING

COMMON BONDS.

School of Chemistry students make soap, probably for a fundraiser, about 1930.

COMMON BONDS

A Memoir in Photographs of the

UNIVERSITY OF MINNESOTA

Andrea Hinding

THE
DONNING COMPANY
PUBLISHERS

The Morris campus mascot,

date unknown.

The Donning Company/Publishers
184 Business Park Drive, Suite 106
Virginia Beach, VA 23462

Steve Mull, *General Manager*
B. L. Walton Jr., *Project Director*
Dawn V. Kofroth, *Assistant General Manager*
Richard A. Horwege, *Senior Editor*
Kevin M. Brown, *Senior Graphic Designer*
James Casper, *Imaging Artist*
Teri S. Arnold, *Senior Marketing Coordinator*

Library of Congress Cataloging-in-Publication Data

Hinding, Andrea.
        Common bonds : a memoir in photographs of the University of Minnesota/
by Andrea Hinding.
                p.   cm.
        Includes bibliographical references.
        ISBN 1-57864-020-2 (hc : alk. paper)
        1. University of Minnesota—History—Pictorial works. I. Title.
LD3353.H56 1998
378.776'579—dc21
                                                              97-42360
                                                                 CIP

Printed in the United States of America

Clarence S. Carter, 1938–1996

For JOHN HOWE
whose imagination, competence,
and commitment to the University
made this book possible;

for TOM SHAUGHNESSY
whose intelligent sympathy
and great personal kindness
helped me finish;

and for CLARENCE CARTER,
semper fi.

CONTENTS

LEFT:

A Jacques Lipchitz sculpture, Solon du Luth, *stands before the Tweed Museum of Art on the Duluth campus, 1967.*

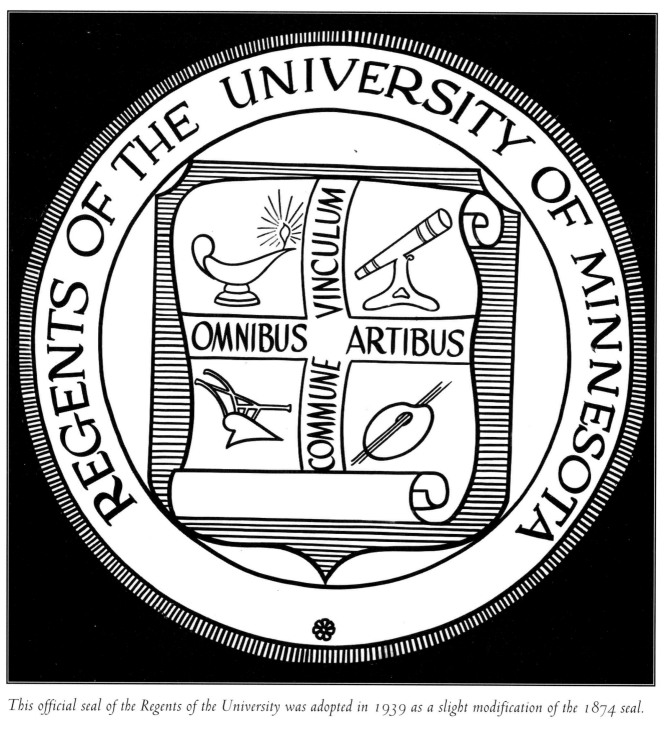

This official seal of the Regents of the University was adopted in 1939 as a slight modification of the 1874 seal.

PREFACE

The Minerva Literary Society, 1905.

W hen the Regents of the University of Minnesota created a new seal in 1874, they took for the school motto an idea borrowed from Cicero, who believed that there existed among all the arts, or branches of learning, a common bond (*Omnibus artibus commune vinculum*). To illustrate the branches of learning the Regents chose a lighted lamp for metaphysical science, a telescope for the physical sciences, an artist's palette for the fine arts, and a plow for applied learning.

This book is an act of remembering, in pictures rather than words, the University of Minnesota. It is also a meditation on bonds, on the forces that have connected rather than divided us. Some bonds are those suggested by the Regents, among the arts and sciences, between classical and applied learning, among disciplines, colleges, and campuses. Others are bonds created by our work and achievements, the efforts of many generations to build an institution for succeeding generations. There is a bond of shared experiences, of compulsory chapel and keggers, of final exams and grant proposals, of the smell of the barns at Crookston and the September walk up the Mall in the Twin Cities, of protests against things as they are. There is the bond created by our symbols and rituals, from Goldy Gopher and the Rouser to commencement ceremonies. There is the bond among those who believe in a world of ideas and invest part of their lives in it, and with others who proudly support their commitment.

We live in a time dominated by competing abstractions and sound bites. On so many issues, education among them, we seem to face each other across chasms, shouting the equivalent of beer commercials—tastes great, less filling, tastes great. . . . I began this book carrying some abstractions of my own, but by the time I had looked at five hundred photographs in the University's archives, they were gone, washed away by the faces of the people of the University. The spirit and title of this book came from their faces and enterprises. So too did a belief, which grew stronger as I worked, that there are important truths about the University that words alone cannot fully convey.

The book begins with a chapter on the wellsprings of the University, by the falls of Saint Anthony and in pioneer life and values. Next are chapters on the familiar tasks of all universities, teaching, research, and service. I have added a chapter on a fourth, unstated task, that of preserving heritage, because we do so much to keep our collective memory and we do it so well. There are chapters on staff members, student life, and physical education; rites and rituals; and some moments of transcendence that cross gender and even species. Next is a chapter acknowledging that our bonds are sometimes weakened by things we do or fail to do or that happen to us. The final chapter, "The Soul of a University," presents nineteen people who embody what is best in University life.

* * *

Those who want to read more about the University's history should begin with James Gray's splendid centennial history, *The University of Minnesota, 1851–1951*. There are also histories of individual campuses, colleges, and programs too numerous to list here. Complete or partial lists can be found through campus libraries and archives.

Photographs from the Crookston, Morris, Duluth, and Waseca campuses are identified as such. All others are from the Twin Cities campus.

Academic officers on the golf course, 1932: (left to right) Lotus D. Coffman, Fred B. Snyder, Guy Stanton Ford,
and William T. Middlebrook. Coffman and Ford were fifth and sixth presidents, respectively, of the University.
Snyder was a regent and Middlebrook, comptroller.

ACKNOWLEDGMENTS

*T*his book rests on the artistry and commitment of photographers who, each with a different eye, have given us a rich visual record of University life. I am deeply grateful to them all but especially to Tom Foley, Ken Moran, Wendell Vandersluis, Gerry Vuchetich, Tom Yuzer, and John Zak. May they continue to record the beauty of what they see, and may we appreciate and reward what they do.

This book is also the product of a wonderful University Library and of generations of librarians and archivists who built it. I am especially indebted to Frank Immler, because he continues to see a library as a "sanctuary of civilization." Thanks also to Cynthia Steinke, Mary Frances Collins, Charlene Mason, Richard Rohrer, and other administrators who understood and supported this project. Maxine B. Clapp and Clodaugh Neiderheiser invested their talent and much of their careers in developing the University Archives; their good work has been continued with equal care and skill by Penelope Krosch and Lois Hendrickson. Many others helped pursue grand ideas and small details, among them Elaine Challacombe, Susan Gangl, Karen Nelson Hoyle, Al Lathrop, Halyna Myroniuk, Don Osier, Patricia Turner, and Joel Wurl. Dave Klaassen and Mark Hammons were, as always, good friends and wise colleagues. Karen Roloson, Sharon Folk, and Ellory Christianson make the Library a better place.

I am grateful that this project gave me an opportunity to see the bonds that link all the University's campuses. At Duluth, Jim Vileta and Pat Maus offered intelligent and gracious service from their large, well-managed collections. Allan Larson and Ardis Thompson shared the heritage of Crookston and their conviction that geography and history matter. Jack Imholte, who proved to be a large part of the collective memory of Morris, and student assistant Tasslyn Frame were remarkable.

People across the University and outside it shared their experiences, offered support, and found elusive facts and images. Among them are Carolyn Allen, Suzanne Baizerman, Robert Bitzan, Margaret Sughrue Carlson, Sis Fenton, Mary Beth Garrigan, Rick Heydinger, Bob Odegard, George Latimer, George Robb, Don Spring, Charlotte Striebel, Masami Suga, John Wallace, Linda Wilson, and Clare Woodward. Rutherford B. Aris and

Allen Goldman struggled valiantly to help an archivist understand science. My good neighbors in the Minnesota Geological Survey, not least G. B. Morey and David Southwick, were outstanding.

Kim Rogers, Elsa Greene, Susan Grigg, Judy Burton Hedin, Lucile M. Kane, Clarke Chambers, and Alice Wilcox enrich this book and my life. So too does the YMCA, whose faith in the good heartens me every day. I could not have undertaken or finished this project without the staff of the Kautz Family YMCA Archives—Dagmar Getz, Dave Carmichael, Joyce Forsgren, and Muriel Griffin. Dagmar's good sense, generosity, and artist's eye fill these pages. In a class by himself is David Holst, whose gifts of coffee, flowers, humor, and sustaining love were constants through it all.

The University Showboat on the Mississippi River, 1958.

ONE

This 1857 sketch by Edwin Whitefield shows the site of the University of Minnesota on the Mississippi River. The village of Saint Anthony is on the right and Minneapolis, on the left. Copyright © 1951 by the University of Minnesota. From James Gray, The University of Minnesota, 1851–1951.

WELLSPRINGS OF THE UNIVERSITY

*I*n 1851, just two years after Minnesota became a territory and before ten thousand white settlers had arrived, the legislature voted to establish "a Territorial institution of learning." Leaders wanted a university that would give Minnesota "a name for intelligence" and improve its chances of quickly becoming a state. They also shared the nineteenth-century conviction, passionately held, that education was the best hope for democracy. And like people

John Sargent Pillsbury, a regent of the University and governor of the state of Minnesota, is portrayed here in an undated engraving. He was one of a group of pioneer leaders who was fiercely determined to build a University worthy of the people of the state. For his years of hard work and remarkable generosity he was known as "the father of the University" and "its most devoted friend."

everywhere, they wanted their children to have the opportunities that education would provide.

The new university began by the Mississippi River, in the village of Saint Anthony, directly across the river from the settlement that would become the city of Minneapolis. After its first site was sold, the second was located nearby, by legislative mandate "at or near the Falls of Saint Anthony." From its place beside the river, the institution of learning grew, adding a farm and a campus in Saint Paul and then campuses in Duluth, Morris, Crookston, and Waseca.

The University of Minnesota draws its character from its place. As the river is central to the Minneapolis campus, the farm and barns and green spaces are to Saint Paul. Crookston is rooted in the Red River Valley and Duluth, in its place on the hills above Lake Superior. Morris is part of the wind-swept western prairie. Waseca, a Dakota word for "land of plenty," grew from rich agricultural soil.

The University takes another part of its identity from agriculture, from life on the land—or vivid memories of parents and grandparents who farmed Minnesota soil. The University of Minnesota is a land-grant school, made possible literally by grants of land from the federal government to the states. These grants ensured that the university would offer education for agriculture, the mechanic arts, and "military affairs" as well as in the classics. The campuses at Saint Paul, Crookston, Morris, and Waseca grew up alongside agricultural experiment stations and secondary schools.

The University of Minnesota is also a state university. It draws its character and much of its historic strength from a long partnership with the people of the state. Citizens of Minnesota sent their children to "the University" to be educated. They added their financial support and their leaders—governors, legislators, regents, publishers, entrepreneurs, and others who cared for and governed the University. In turn the University offered the fruits of research and contemplation. It educated citizens in the liberal arts and trained them to practice medicine and the law, pharmacy, and social work. It trained them to teach and to heal.

As the world inevitably changes, so too will the state and its university. New sources of strength and identity are added, but these will always rest on the older ones, on the place where the University stands and on its past.

Old Main, the first grand University building and the symbol of pioneer hopes for beauty and permanence, is beautifully portrayed in this artist's woodcut. Erected in 1858 at a cost that nearly bankrupted the still-young school, Old Main was famous for its forty-three wood-burning stoves and lack of ventilation. The building was destroyed by fire in 1904. Copyright © 1909 by the University of Minnesota. From E. Bird Johnson, Forty Years of the University of Minnesota.

The School of Agriculture's Class of 1912 holds commencement exercises. The school, established in the Twin Cities in 1888 to train young men and women for "life on the land," offered general education and agricultural training to students who already had a "good common school education" and practical farm experience. Classes for the two-year course met from October to April, seasons when pupils could be spared from the farm. In Minnesota schools of agriculture grew up near University agriculture experiment stations.

NO PALM WITHOU

THE DUST OF LABOR.

The Morris School for Indians, seen here in an undated photo, was established by the Sisters of Mercy in 1887. The Sisters ran the school until 1897, when the federal government took over and turned it into an industrial school for Native Americans. In 1909, after policy changed again, pupils were returned to their reservations for education. In 1910 the school was replaced by the West Central School of Agriculture and Experiment Station. In 1960 Morris became a University campus.

The library of the State Normal School at Duluth is shown here in 1902. Normal schools were created in the nineteenth century to train teachers, primarily for elementary schools. The Duluth school opened in 1902, and in 1921, as two-year normal schools were being replaced by four-year teachers colleges, it became the State Teachers College. The "College on the Hill" joined the University in 1947.

Railroad builder James J. Hill speaks at Hill Day at Crookston in the Red River Valley, probably 1908. When Hill gave land for a University agriculture experiment station there in 1895, he asked that a school be established to teach the results of experimentation, and in 1906 the Northwest School of Agriculture opened. Founded on "faith in the Valley," the school trained citizen-leaders for education, research, and service. In 1966 Crookston became a campus of the University.

University of Minnesota

Technical College-Waseca

Waseca, a Dakota word for "land of plenty," was home to a University agriculture experiment station and the Southern School of Agriculture. It opened as a University campus in 1971 to "train semi-professional people for the broad field of agriculture"; its motto was "This Place Is for Kids." The Waseca campus was closed in 1992. These photos show an aerial view of the campus about 1971, and the Student Senate in 1986.

TWO

ABOVE AND RIGHT:

These honors scholars in Greek, from the Class of 1901, were taught by Jabez Brooks. Brooks, pictured about 1888, was a member of the University's first faculty and taught Greek from 1869 to 1909.

TEACHING AND LEARNING

A university is a place where people gladly teach and gladly learn. We come together to discover philosophy and medicine, to teach method and point of view, to read the literature of a profession or understand the structure of a discipline. In the vital work of education, faculties are assembled, a curriculum is designed, degree requirements are established. Students enroll to earn degrees and prepare for adult life, to earn the right to enter a profession or a life of the mind.

Members of the faculty of the College of Education, 1910.

RIGHT:
Members of the faculty of the School of Mines, 1910.

And there is more, for much of teaching and learning is not confined to content and method, nor bound by time and place. Students also learn about passion and curiosity in a Chinese history lecture course, about humility and ambiguity in a science lab, about ego and pique in seminar games. In chemistry and calculus many have discovered the nature and limits of their minds; others found them in creative writing and Proust. Faculty members learn as they teach, never more than the first times they give a course. Later they learn about the intractable parts of human nature, about frustration as a class goes from bad to worse,

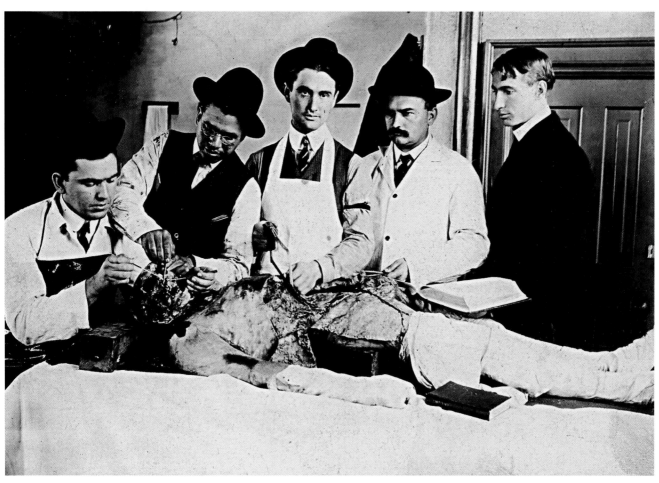

A dissection in an anatomy class, about 1902.

Thomas Sandler Roberts (front row) sits with students in his bird class, 1919. Roberts, a physician and professor of pediatrics, gave up medicine to study and teach ornithology. He wrote the classic Birds of Minnesota *and directed the Museum of Natural History for thirty years.*

about the limits of language and how hard it can be to convey what is important.

Teaching has its own complexities. As we commonly use the word, teaching is straightforward, almost unilateral: one teaches, one learns. In reality teaching is inseparable from learning, and it is as much about exploring, provoking, and leading as it is about conveying the facts of nutrition and the methods of anthropology. It is being the occasion of a student's entering the world of ideas or discovering love of truth. It is entrusting to the next generation the science or language one loves.

Some of teaching and learning has changed over a century. More students enroll in graduate or professional

Students participate in a short course in bee culture, about 1922.

Clockwise from upper left are students taking the Cooperative General Culture Test, 1940; in a classroom, 1946; taking a test, 1933; and studying in the old library in Burton Hall, 1922.

Clockwise from upper left are Fletcher Martin (standing) teaching an art workshop at Duluth, 1954 (Photo by Barney Thomas); Truman Tilleraas (right) teaching about dairy cattle judging at Crookston, no date; Arthur Naftalin (who later served as mayor of Minneapolis) teaching a political science class, Fieldwork in Government and Politics, 1952; and students in a class on motors and tractor operations at Crookston, 1955.

studies, or as adults, and more feel the pressure to find a way to earn a living. Faculty members feel pressures, internal and imposed, to contribute more through their research. Mastery of a subject seems ever more elusive.

Not all is always glad. But still the joy in the awakening persists. Knowing enough of literature to find an echo of Mark Twain in James Joyce, showing a student the bird's capacity to heal, finding love of the law, seeing the beauty of nature's randomness for the first time—these are the best gifts and rewards of education.

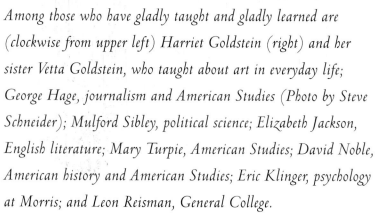

*Among those who have gladly taught and gladly learned are
(clockwise from upper left) Harriet Goldstein (right) and her
sister Vetta Goldstein, who taught about art in everyday life;
George Hage, journalism and American Studies (Photo by Steve
Schneider); Mulford Sibley, political science; Elizabeth Jackson,
English literature; Mary Turpie, American Studies; David Noble,
American history and American Studies; Eric Klinger, psychology
at Morris; and Leon Reisman, General College.*

Students participate in a Medical School program for disadvantaged students, 1976.

Horace Bond, an instructor in theatre arts in the 1970s, taught courses on black drama and the black man in the American theatre, in part to offset the legacy of minstrel shows. Photo by John Ryan.

Harry Reasoner talks with journalism students in 1970, the year the Regents gave him an Outstanding Achievement Award. In 1989 he was awarded an honorary bachelor's degree.

Eugene Savage (center) participates
in the Indian Mental Health Training
Project at Duluth, 1980.

RIGHT:
Students enjoy a Business
Administration class in small
business management, date unknown.

A summer institute class in South Asian Studies, 1969.

Philosophy professor Burnham Terrell converses with students on the Mall, about 1965.

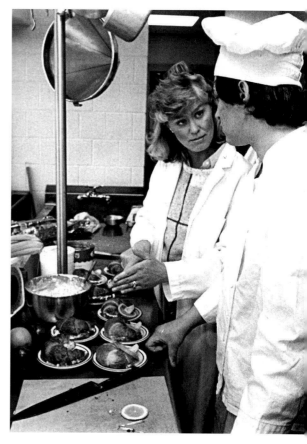

Nancy Johnson Nelson welcomes on-the-job training in a hospitality management class at Crookston, 1984.

Nils Hasselmo, professor of Scandinavian languages and literature and president of the University, tutors a student, about 1982.

Roy Schuessler, a voice teacher, singer,
and member of the music faculty, works
at the piano in 1975.

Duluth students concentrate on their
work in a 1971 ceramics class and in
a 1987 chemistry laboratory.

THREE

The houseboat Megalops *was built for the University at Mankato and used to survey fauna, "especially the fishes," in the Minnesota and Mississippi Rivers from Mankato to Red Wing. It is seen here with its skiff* Zoea, *about 1899.*

SEEKING KNOWLEDGE AND UNDERSTANDING

*I*n 1948 Raymond Gibson, the first chancellor of the new University campus at Duluth, explained to the Rotary Club there how the Duluth curriculum was organized. We live in a physical universe from which we cannot escape, Gibson said, and so we study the sciences. We also live in a human society from which we rarely escape, and so we study the social sciences. And each of us, he said, lives in a body, with a consciousness from which we escape only in death,

An experiment in drying nursery corn at the Agriculture Experiment Station, about 1901.

and so we study the arts and the humanities, to understand better our human condition.

Like the Duluth curriculum, the research mission of the University is nothing more, and nothing less, than understanding our world and ourselves. We may seek knowledge for its own sake, because to know is better than not to know, and we sometimes pursue it out of simple curiosity. More often, though, we seek knowledge to provide comfort and security for ourselves and others. We learn how—and why—to dry corn and isolate the gene that causes cystic fibrosis, and we think about why phrases from Shakespeare and Bach echo in so many human hearts.

Minnesota farmer Wendelin Grimm (seen here with Mrs. Grimm, date unknown) established a legendary variety of alfalfa that could survive northern winters.

Left to right in 1924 are Walter C. Coffey, A. B. Lyman, and Andrew Boss examining the original alfalfa field.

For many generations, from those who counted the species of fish in the Minnesota River to those who contemplate theories of mathematics a century later, the faculty, staff, and students of the University have added to a body of knowledge that is humanity's great hedge against the darkness of ignorance, hunger, disease, and despair. That hard-won

Arthur G. Ruggles (right, date unknown), professor of entomology, camped out in a grasshopper-infested field during the summer of 1923 to test poisons. From what he learned he built an eradication program estimated to have saved fifty million dollars in crops in 1932 and 1933. A "Mr. Strand" (above) demonstrates the gas mask and air gun used to spray "hoppers" in 1931.

knowledge yields more than hardier azaleas and ductile ceramics. It also helps deepen our understanding, and occasionally it offers glimpses of the wisdom that we need to complete our finite lives.

Edward W. "Bud" Davis tests paving blocks for the School of Mines Experiment Station in 1935. Davis, an engineer who devoted thirty-five years to finding ways to utilize low-grade iron ores, was better known as "Mr. Taconite."

Jean Piccard's balloon, launched from Northrop field in 1936, traveled six hundred miles before it landed in the Ozark Mountains. It provided data about the stratosphere, the upper portion of the earth's atmosphere. Jeannette Piccard (center) piloted balloons with her husband, a faculty member in aeronautical engineering.

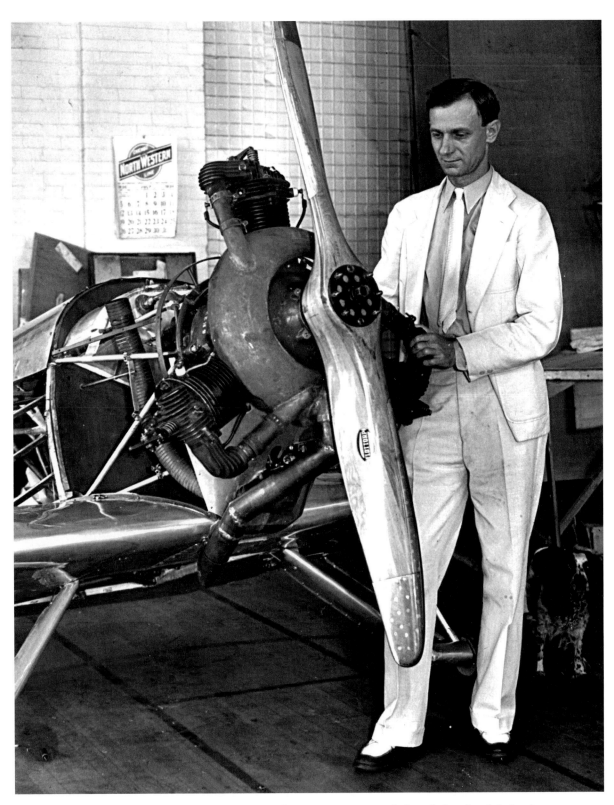

Aeronautical engineer John D. Akerman, seen here in 1936, founded and then headed the department of aeronautical engineering for thirty years. He specialized in "airplane design and construction." His "Tailless Aircraft" was donated to the Smithsonian Institution in 1970.

Members of the Medical School faculty (1939), J. C. McKinley (seated) with (left to right) Wesley W. Spink, Leo G. Rigler, and E. T. Bell, test a "psycho-galvanometer" on a patient "suspected of untruthfulness."

RIGHT:
J. William Buchta, a physicist and pioneer in science education and the liberal arts honors program, checks out his "ashcan radium detector" about 1932.

Alfred O. C. Nier works with the mass spectroscope he used to isolate a sample of uranium-235, about 1940. Nier, who enrolled at the University in 1927, when he was sixteen, went on to become Regents' professor of physics. His work helped open the Atomic Age.

Albin W. Johnson (top), dairy products supervisor, makes Minnesota Blue Cheese in 1947. "Minnesota Blue," made from the milk of cows and ripened in sandstone caves along the Mississippi River, was developed at the University.

"Old Battler" was a monkey used in polio research, about 1949.

56

COMMON BONDS: *A Memoir in Photographs of the* UNIVERSITY OF MINNESOTA

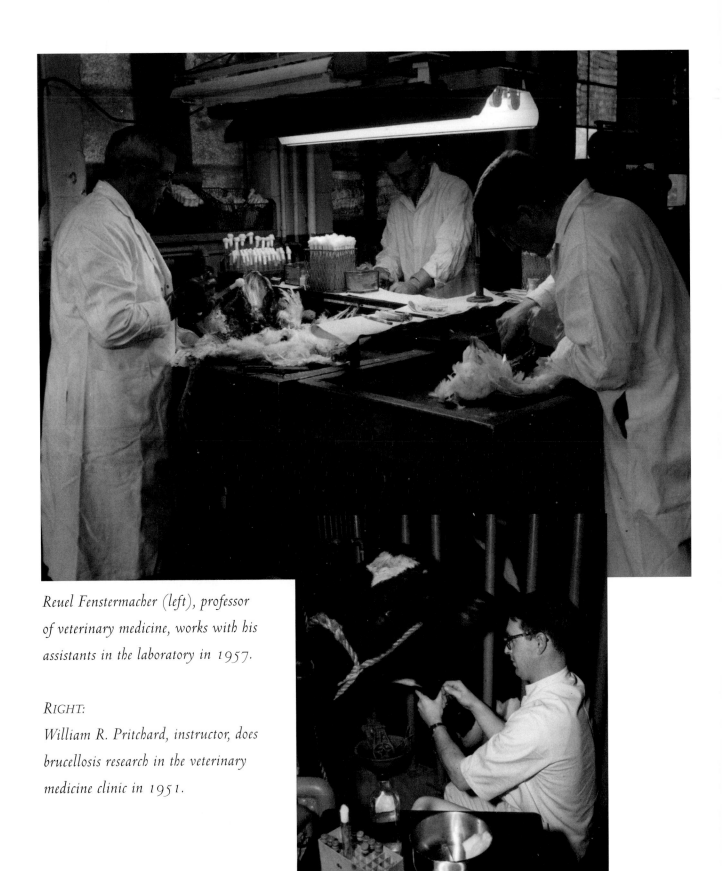

Reuel Fenstermacher (left), professor of veterinary medicine, works with his assistants in the laboratory in 1957.

RIGHT:
William R. Pritchard, instructor, does brucellosis research in the veterinary medicine clinic in 1951.

Herbert Feigl, Regents' professor of philosophy, 1966. Photo by Best.

Lawrence Markus, Regents' professor of mathematics, about 1992.

Dominick Argento, Regents' professor of music, 1976.

Gisela Konopka, professor of social work, 1953.

John Najarian, physician, healer, and clinical professor in surgery, about 1985.

Vasilikie Demos, associate professor of sociology on the Morris campus, date unknown.

Elvin Stakman, professor of plant pathology, date unknown.

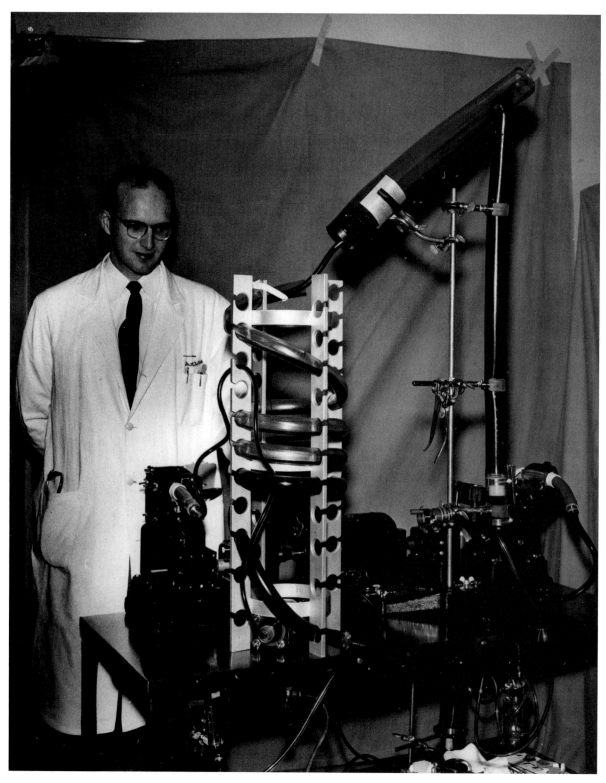

Richard A. DeWall, resident in surgery, observes his "bubble oxygenator" in 1958. DeWall developed the machine to keep oxygen in a patient's blood during surgery.

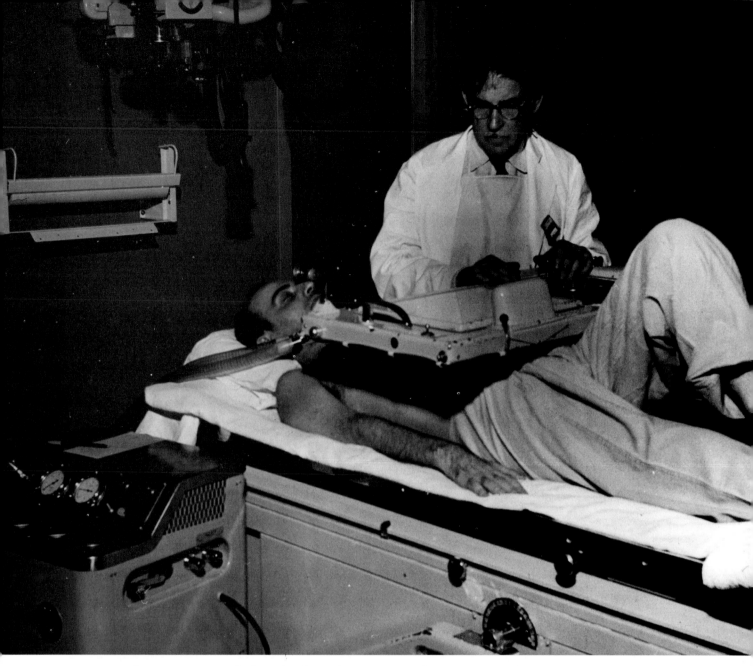

Leo G. Rigler, professor of radiology, works with a patient in the Van Bergen respirator in 1955. Rigler was a pioneer in using x-rays to diagnose and treat chest diseases and cancers.

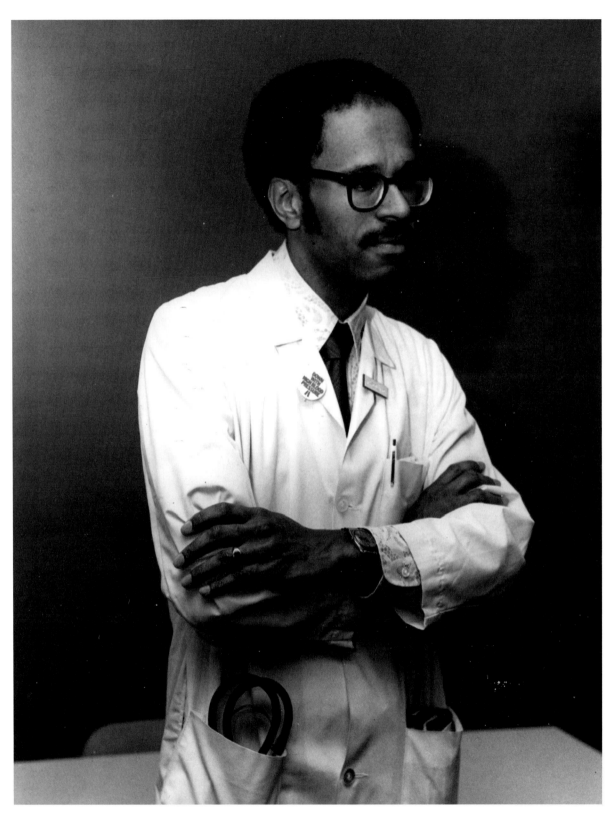

Richard F. Gillum, seen here in 1978, was a faculty member in medicine and public health. Gillum studied hypertension, cardiovascular disease, and patient compliance. During his years at the University he contributed a health column to the Twin Cities Courier, *an African-American newspaper.*

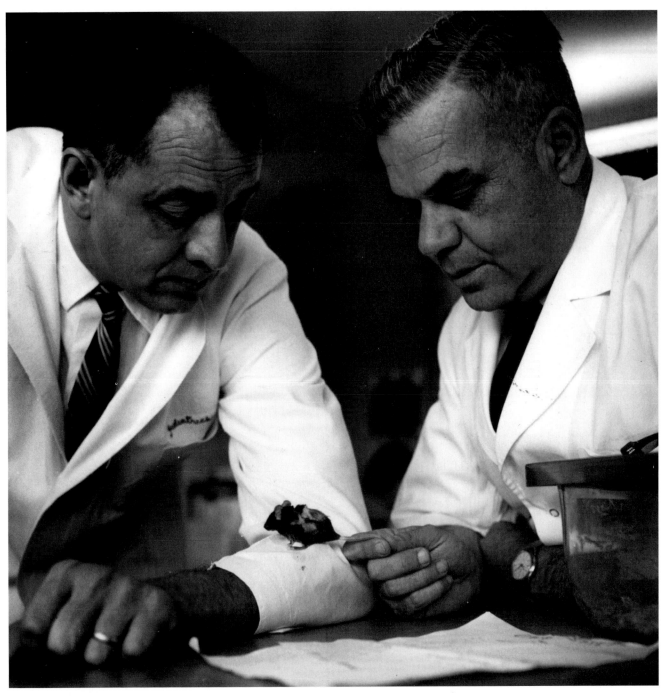

Cancer researchers Robert A. Good (right) and Carlos Martinez are seen here in 1963. Good, a Regents'
professor of medicine, pioneered in bone-marrow transplants. Martinez, a native of Argentina and a faculty
member from 1951 until his death in 1966, studied hormonal factors in cancer and immunological barriers
in transplants.

Katherine Nash, sculptor and studio arts professor, confers with visiting professor David Tolerton in 1965. Nash was an early sculptor in metal and a pioneer in the use of direct metal welding.

Professor of philosophy Marcia Eaton, seen here in 1994, works in the field of aesthetics and helps us understand what art is and what it is not.

FOUR

Farmers' Institutes, which carried news of "agricultural experimentation" across the state, were founded by Oren Gregg. He is seated at center of this Farmers' Institute Corps staff portrait, about 1890.

EXTENSIONS

*B*efore the University had graduated its first students, local farmers turned to it for advice about their crops and soils. In doing so, they opened a traffic in ideas and skills and needs and interests that has flowed, for more than a century now, between the people of the state and their University.

We eventually defined that traffic as the extension, service, or outreach mission of the University, though the very concept of a "mission" and the names for it seem inadequate to describe something so mutual and inevitable. Collectively and over time, out of such particulars as wheat rust and locusts, we built an educational purpose. We built it partly from democratic theories and practical politics, but even more so from conversations, small courtesies, and the instinct to solve problems—from mending an eagle's broken wing to finding a way to offer a class in Cambridge or North Branch.

Over a century the community served and serving has broadened. Ideas flow now along superhighway and information highway rather than by "good-seed" special trains and county fair exhibits. Classes can be extended by television and the Internet as well as by sending faculty

University extension trains, such as this one about 1911, carried short courses to farmers across the state.

members and their courses across the state. But the spilling-over of talent and concern, the partnership in defining needs, the urge to put knowledge "at the service of the community" remains, unchanged.

Martin County's extension project exhibit at the Minnesota State Fair, 1930.

Stewart Thomson's program "Your Health and You" was broadcast on University station KUOM for twenty years. Thomson, seen at the microphone in 1952, was equally famous for his required course in public health.

Minnesota's first broadcasting station "9X1," in the department of electrical engineering, is seen here in 1920, the year it began broadcasting weather reports. In 1945 it became KUOM, the "University of the Air."

BELOW:

William A. O'Brien talks with children on his WCCO radio program, about 1945. For his work in public medical education, O'Brien was called "Doctor to a Million" and "missionary to the whole state." Photo by Bruce Sifford Studio.

This is the fabled dental clinic in Owre Hall in 1948, a year when dental students and staff filled thirteen thousand cavities.

RIGHT PAGE:

Credit union leaders at the Nolte Center for Continuing Education, 1959.

Shari Kirchoff, a patient in the speech-and-hearing clinic at Duluth, 1960.

A tutorial on the Duluth campus, 1978.

Dental Hygiene's "Project Toothbrush," 1970.

Stanley Sahlstrom listens to Jami Clark Nelson during Aggie Spring at Crookston, 1990. Sahlstrom was first provost at Crookston and served as a member of the Board of Regents from 1985 to 1997.

Ernie Hillukka, member of the Dairy Herd Improvement Association, listens to George Marx, professor of animal science, during Forage Day at Crookston, 1986. Photo by Gene Miller.

Judith A. Brooks (right) converses with a visitor at the 1985 Bologna Children's Book Fair in Italy. Brooks gave money to support "An American Sampler," an exhibit of materials from the Kerlan Collection of Children's Literature. Photo by Karen Nelson Hoyle.

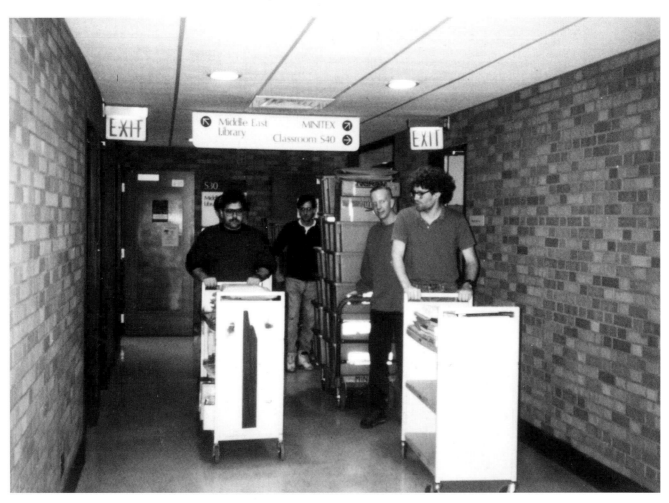

Students work for MINITEX (the Minnesota Interlibrary Teletype Exchange) in 1993. MINITEX was started in the 1960s to share library resources with the state and region. Through it the University Library lends more material than any other library in the country. Photo by Kathleen Drozd.

Reatha Clark King, president of the General Mills Foundation, releases a bald eagle who had been a patient at the University's Raptor Center. The release took place on Martin Luther King's birthday in 1992.

James Ford Bell, University alumnus and regent and founder of General Mills, is shown in 1953 with the 1667 Blaeu Atlas, *part of his collection of rare books about European discovery and exploration which he gave to the University.*

This place of memory has been built by the acts of thousands of people: librarians who devote careers to building research collections in art history or American literature, a historian preserving endangered records of social reform in the United States, a curator boxing up architectural records kept in an old shack while the bulldozer waiting to demolish the building idled outside. Alumni have added single homecoming buttons or an old issue of the *Daily* and citizen-collectors offer treasures accumulated over a lifetime.

No one decided to make the University a place of memory. It became one because of the nature of its work and its traditions. It became one because of the people who are

For thirty years librarian Patricia Turner has collected scores, photographs, recordings, and other objects that document the African-American spiritual. Pictured here is the Fisk University Jubilee Quartet and two of its recordings of "Swing Low, Sweet Chariot."

The Morris campus student Jazz Ensemble, 1989.

The Frederick R. Weisman Art Museum, seen here in 1993, embodies President Lotus Coffman's "dream of long-standing," his desire that everyone have access "to the things that make life worth living, to the cultural inheritances of the human race."

A tablet from the facade of Memorial Stadium is lifted to safety just before the old football stadium was demolished in 1992. Five tablets of Indiana limestone from above the ceremonial entrance were preserved to remember the stadium that had been an important part of our "shared identity."

Cheng-Khee Chee, a watercolorist, teacher, and librarian at the Duluth campus, paints in 1987. Cheng-Khee's work combines and synthesizes elements of Oriental and Western philosophy, style, and technique.

Photographer Tom Foley displays an image from his 1989 exposition,
"A Picture Is Worth a Thousand People." Foley, seen here in 1994,
has been campus photographer since 1973. Photo by Elizabeth Foley.

Photographers whose work documents University life (clockwise from top left): Warner Clapp (right) with Kenning Hollis, 1948; Ken Moran, Duluth alumnus and campus photographer for forty years, 1987 (Photo by Lucy Kragness); Gerry Vuchetich, since 1984 photographer for women's intercollegiate athletics; and Wendell Vandersluis, since 1969 photographer for men's intercollegiate athletics, 1993.

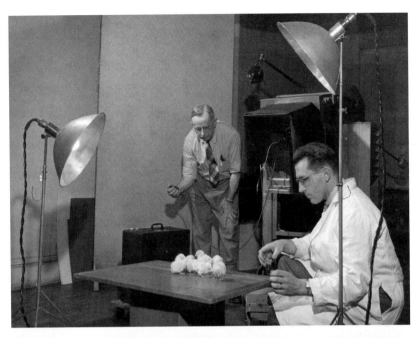

University archivist Maxine B. Clapp (left), 1953, and assistant archivist Clodaugh Neiderheiser (above), 1976, preserved the University's records and with them much of its heritage. Neiderheiser identified and cataloged thousands of photographs, including many in this book.

James Gray, historian, critic, and novelist, poses by the Minnesota Room in 1950. Gray wrote the centennial history of the University.

SIX

President Cyrus Northrop stands front and center with members of the administrative staff of the University in 1910.

BACKBONE OF THE UNIVERSITY

*J*ohn Henry Cardinal Newman once said that all that is required to have a university is a faculty and a library. Cardinal Newman lived in a simpler time, and he didn't know Ken Moran and Ardis Thompson and Barb Foster.

Since the University opened, its faculty and students have been joined and supported by a third group, civil service and other staff members who shovel coal, fix broken water pipes, answer reference questions, write software programs,

Ralph Waldo "Skipper" Spencer, conductor of the intercampus streetcar, punches a ticket in 1933. Spencer changed his given names because of his admiration for Ralph Waldo Emerson and the English philosopher Herbert Spencer.

Mrs. M. Frances Pierce, graduate school secretary, talks with Chinese graduate student Cheng Teh-Peng in 1939.

University telephone switchboard operators, 1949.

Nels Thompson, upholsterer, ties springs on a chair in 1951.

Margaret J. Salisbury at the purchasing desk, 1952.

Albert Ulsby, senior general mechanic, works at his lathe in 1957.

Members of the Coffman Memorial Union staff, 1941.

Below:
Heating plant staff members unload coal in 1947.

Ardis Thompson, secretary in External Relations for the Crookston campus, 1994.

William F. Maupins, science laboratory supervisor for the Duluth campus, 1963.

Barb Foster, office administrator in General College, 1993.

SEVEN

Members of the Lambda chapter of Delta Gamma sit
for a studio portrait at the University about 1889.

Members of the Alpha Sigma chapter of Sigma Chi
pose at their University house in 1890.

STUDENT LIVES

F or students, much of University life is lived outside the classroom, the library, and the laboratory. For students University life is also the smell of the barns at Crookston during spring melt and "moldy old Walter" in August, the wind whipping off Lake Superior or across the Minnesota prairie. It is dormitory food, cafeteria lines, and vending machine "coffee," the frustrations of closed classes and library fines or the good luck of finding a cheap place to park and a quiet place to study. Student life is cutting up,

At the 1923 Junior Livestock Show in South Saint Paul, Gladys Lund shows off her geese and Ray Brynglson Calloway, his roosters. William Scheilke of Beltrami County poses with his Shropshire lamb at the 1939 Minnesota State Fair. T. A. "Dad" Erickson, a University faculty member and father of 4-H Clubs in Minnesota, helped stage animal shows and competitions for boys and girls across the state.

acting out, challenging authority. It is affiliation—finding friends in a fraternity or sorority or at the YMCA.

Much of student life, or at least the accidents of student life, has changed over a century. Grumbling about the stewed tomatoes and creamed corn has yielded to complaints about the burgers and the fries. The "gumbo" of the old roads at Crookston has been paved over, permanently, by an interstate freeway. The rhythms of the school year are governed less by the rhythms of the land, and students travel to the University not only from Graceville and Holdingford but from Taiwan and Tanzania. Still, there are constants in this life, the important constants of being young, of trying to find meaning and a place in the world, of trying to find a way to make a living and a life. In them we can all find enduring richness and wonder.

Students celebrate at a meal in Sanford Hall in 1941.

Students line up at the "Ag" Union cafeteria on the Saint Paul campus in 1945.

The University Quiz Bowl team waits in the Murphy Hall auditorium to hear questions from quizmaster Allen Ludden in New York City, 1953. The team won eight consecutive matches before losing to Brown University.

Freshmen at Welcome Week, 1956.

Students listen intently at a convocation on the Duluth campus, 1971.

RIGHT:

Student leaders Rose Mary Freeman and Horace Huntley take their stand together during a student protest in Morrill Hall, 1969. Minneapolis Tribune *photo.*

COMMON BONDS: *A Memoir in Photographs of the* UNIVERSITY OF MINNESOTA

Parking on the River Flats, 1965.

Students on the Mall, 1970. Minneapolis Tribune *photo.*

Students have fun (clockwise from upper left) on the Waseca campus, 1986; at Crookston, date unknown; and in General College, 1989.

Students gather in the Kirby Center on the Duluth campus, 1982.

At home in a Crookston campus dorm, 1982.

Freshman Kelly Krueger ends a long day on the Crookston campus, date unknown.

EIGHT

The Gopher baseball team, 1888.

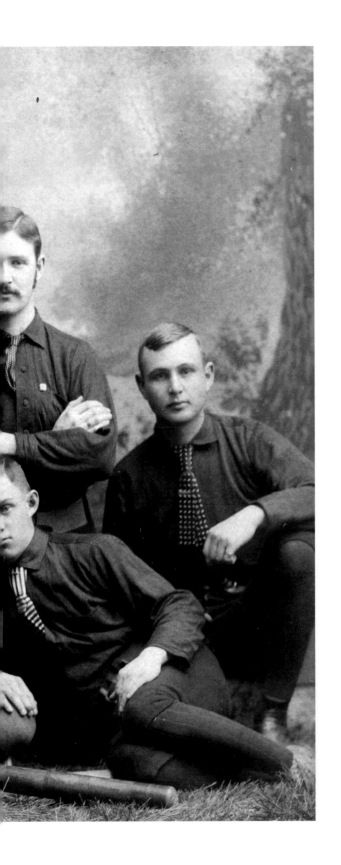

PHYSICAL EDUCATION

*T*he University's first student-athletes played their games more innocently, roughhousing on unfinished fields, finding their opponents among classmates at the University or at neighboring schools. Over the decades, as playing fields and equipment improved and competition intensified and became national, college sport lost some of its innocence. With the privilege of being the most visible symbol of the University came the burdens of winning and of revenue.

What has changed far less is what student-athletes learn in sport. On playing fields and in the gym they learn skill, discipline, concentration, teamwork, and friendship. They find coaches to teach them and to grieve losses with them. On rare occasions they are rewarded with a moment's mastery, a perfect backhand or takedown. The luckiest find enduring affection for their games and the people who play them.

The Class of 1907's women's basketball team, 1904.

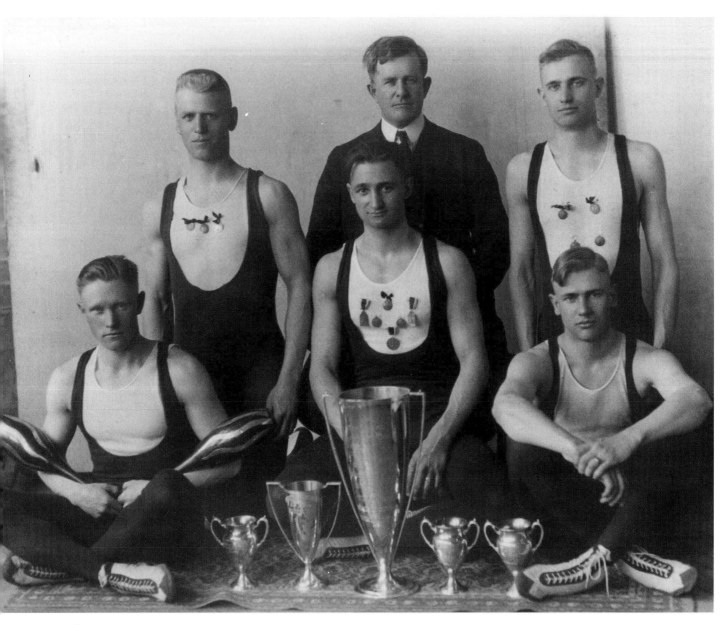

The gymnastics team, 1921.

Roy Griak, seen here in 1975, coached the men's track and cross-country teams for thirty-three years.

Dick Siebert, "The Chief" who coached Gopher baseball for thirty years, makes his point with student-athlete Dave Winfield in 1971. Winfield was drafted in three professional sports and had a long career in major-league baseball. Photo by Paul Wychor.

Crookston teammates, 1975.

The Morris basketball team celebrates a victory over Winona in 1993. Photo by Jesse Bartz.

Swimmer Jo Elsen hugs a teammate, about 1984.

While these rites and rituals accomplish their specific purposes, they also satisfy other abiding human needs. They bring us together to enrich our common life. They provide us an occasion to dress up—to don cap and gown or pin on a corsage. They let us show respect for form and civility. They remind us that we are part of something larger and much older, an institution and tradition that help anchor our civilization.

Harry Suzzalo (right), University of Washington president, joins Lotus Coffman (left), University president, and William Folwell, president emeritus, at commencement in June 1927.

RIGHT:
Marshals head the 1965 procession on Cap and Gown Day, when seniors traditionally first donned their caps and gowns to march up the Mall.

COMMON BONDS: *A Memoir in Photographs of the* UNIVERSITY OF MINNESOTA

Carl T. Rowan, Minnesota journalist, speaks at the inauguration of Malcolm Moos as tenth president of the University in 1968. The students behind Rowan had occupied the Northrop Auditorium stage as part of a protest.

RIGHT:

C. Peter Magrath speaks in Northrop Auditorium during his inauguration as eleventh president of the University in 1974.

Earl Brown is at left with a shovel at the groundbreaking for the Garden City residential community project on the Brown farm in 1956.

RIGHT:
Ribbon-cutting on the Waseca campus, date unknown.

COMMON BONDS: A Memoir in Photographs of the UNIVERSITY OF MINNESOTA

Actress Loretta Young cuts the ribbon at the opening of the Variety Club Heart Hospital, 1951. Variety clubs, which were composed of entertainers, raised funds for the Hospital. At Young's right is President James Morrill.

Participants in the 1956 Hospital Drive for the Masonic Memorial Hospital gather around the punch bowl.

Business Office staff members enjoy a staff luncheon, 1948.

Clara Brown Arny (left), professor of home economics education, receives the University's Outstanding Achievement Award from Regent Marjorie Howard in 1958. The award was given during the College of Education Alumni Association's annual dinner.

Olive Crosthwait, University alumna, pharmacist, and businesswoman, receives the Outstanding Achievement Award from President James Morrill at the Minnesota State Pharmaceutical Association convention, 1956.

Couples display their affection (clockwise from upper left) on the Morris campus, 1981; in 1973 (photo by John Ryan); and at Cap and Gown Day, 1954.

GREAT PERFORMANCES

*S*ometimes in our all-too imperfect world, things go right and we have a chance to celebrate. The field goal splits the uprights, the turkey is declared best in the state, the music is so full of magic that listeners are transformed.

Such feats are not accidents, not the product of luck or of the moment. They arise from talent, discipline, imagination, and commitment over a long time, even a lifetime. In them we usually find principle or a sense of duty, obligation to family,

Frank Bencriscutto, director of University bands, conducts in Novosibersk, 1969.

RIGHT:

The Concert Band performs in Siberia, 1969.

BELOW:

After the tour, the Concert Band played a Command Performance in the White House Rose Garden, where President Richard Nixon and his wife Pat sat beside President Malcolm Moos and his wife Tracy to listen.

In a sea of endowed chairs are (left to right) Curtis L. Carlson, Governor Rudy Perpich, and President Ken Keller, about 1987. Carlson, a Minnesota business executive and philanthropist, was national campaign chairman of the University's Minnesota Campaign, which raised $364 million and endowed 110 faculty chairs. When it concluded in 1987, it was the most successful fundraising effort ever by a public university.

ELEVEN

DISCONTINUITIES

LEFT:

Arthur Upson (date unknown), University faculty member and promising young American poet, died by drowning at age thirty-one.

Some of the photographs in this chapter are painful to look at and think about, for they bring us face to face with parts of the human condition and of University life that it is easier simply to avoid.

Some of these images document a loss—the death of a gifted and troubled young poet and the burning of a historic building. One asks us to look directly into the face of racism. Others remind us that in war some good people look for enemies in places they don't ordinarily find them,

William Schaper, head of the political science department, was dismissed by the Board of Regents in 1917. The Regents decided that Schaper's opposition to World War I made him unfit to fulfill his duties as a faculty member. In 1938, after adopting a strong statement of support for academic freedom, the Regents made Schaper a professor emeritus and awarded him his salary for 1917–1918.

Forrest O. Wiggins, seen here in 1947, was instructor of philosophy, and the first full-time African-American faculty member. His public questioning of the social order brought criticism of the University. In 1951 President James Morrill overturned the recommendation of the Philosophy Department that Wiggins be granted tenure and terminated his appointment.

"Old Main," a landmark of the Duluth campus, was destroyed by fire in 1993.

Workers demolish Memorial Stadium in 1992.

Commencement ceremonies for the twentieth and last graduating class at the Waseca campus were held in June 1992.

It was Acting Chancellor Nan Wilhelmson's duty to close the Waseca campus in 1992.

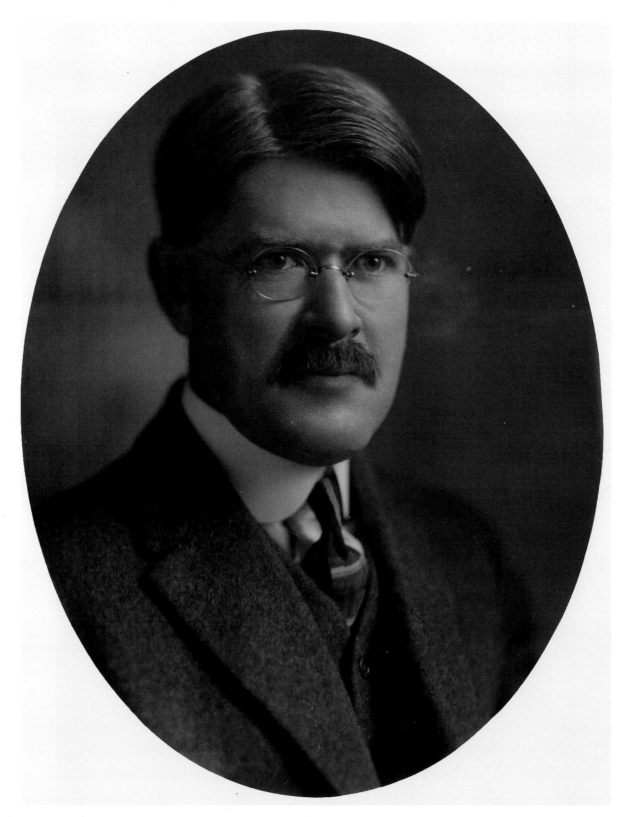

Elias Potter Lyon (1915), was a leader in medical education, professor of physiology, and dean of the Medical School from 1913 to 1936. Lyon believed that the basis of the scientific ideal is "the love of truth" and that the ideal is best expressed in an imperative, "Prove all things."

Common Bonds: A Memoir in Photographs of the University of Minnesota

J. Anna Norris (1925) was a physician and director of physical education for women from 1912 to 1941. Norris, who earned her medical degree from Northwestern University after being refused admission to medical schools at Harvard and Tufts Universities, used her medical knowledge in testing and diagnosis of student health. She worked for physical education facilities, programs for women, and a student health service.

Alverta Mae Phillips (1919), who lived in Saint Paul, received her bachelor's degree from the College of Science, Literature, and the Arts in 1919. She was a member of the University's Equal Suffrage Association, Women's Self-Government Association, and Tam o' Shanter, a social club.

Everett Fraser (1925), a Canadian by birth, was professor of law and dean of the Law School from 1920 to 1948. Fraser helped broaden legal education so that students would improve the law as well as practice it. Above all else, he wanted attorneys to have "the spirit of public service."

Betty Sullivan, who was born in Minneapolis, received her bachelor's degree in chemistry in 1922 and her Ph.D. in biochemistry in 1935. In 1922 she began her long career as a biochemist and executive at the Russell Miller Milling Company (later the Peavey and Conagra Companies). She remains grateful to the University, she has said, because it gave her "teachers, science, and many friends."

William James Mayo (1924), a physician at Rochester's Mayo Clinic, served as a member of the Board of Regents from 1907 to 1939. "In every branch of study he insisted upon three things—directness, democracy, and research."

Frederick Wulling (about 1934) was professor of pharmacology, director of the medicinal plant garden, and dean of the College of Pharmacy from 1892 to 1936. Wulling also earned two degrees in law, played the violin, collected art and rare books, and helped found the Minneapolis Institute of Arts. Of his contributions he said: "I merely saw my duty and did it as well as my ability permitted."

COMMON BONDS: *A Memoir in Photographs of the* UNIVERSITY OF MINNESOTA

Olga Lakela (1956), a native of Finland who received her master's and Ph.D. degrees from the University, was professor of botany and curator of the herbarium at the Duluth State Teachers College (later the University of Minnesota Duluth) from 1935 to 1958. At Duluth, Lakela gathered and documented thirty thousand plant specimens from the Arrowhead region. After she retired, she worked at the University of South Florida, Tampa, where she helped collect one hundred thousand specimens for a tropical Florida herbarium.

LEFT:

Helen Canoyer (1952), the first woman to earn a Ph.D. in economics at the University of Minnesota, was a member of the faculty of the School of Business Administration from 1929 to 1953. She was expert on personal and family financial planning and lectured on "What Every Woman Should Know About Money." She left the University in 1953 to be dean of home economics at Cornell University.

John Berryman (date unknown) was Regents' professor of humanities and a Pulitzer Prize–winning poet whose long struggle with "our very moment in human trouble" ended in suicide in 1972. He was remembered by one former student as "the superb teacher searching for meaning."

Faith Thompson (about 1938) received her bachelor's, master's, and Ph.D. degrees from the University where she taught history for nearly forty years. Thompson devoted most of her life to the study of the Magna Carta, which she described as the oldest of the "liberty documents." When her major work, twenty-five years in the making, was published, a colleague said, with respect and sympathy: "So much labor has it cost."

RIGHT:

O. Meredith Wilson (date unknown), historian and ninth president of the University, believed that "the business of liberal education in a democracy is to make free men wise."

Lloyd "Snapper" Stein (date unknown) applied more than five million feet of tape to student athletes during more than forty years as men's athletic trainer. Stein, who took other part-time jobs so that he could afford to stay at the University, was once asked why he hadn't accepted a better-paying position that had been offered. There are "experiences I have had in this training room that can't be compensated with money," he explained.

George Morrison (1976), a member of the Grand Portage band of the Minnesota Chippewa and "an American artist," was a member of the studio arts faculty from 1970 to 1983. The most important thing I tell students, he said, is that "each has to make his or her own search" and "try to arrive at an honest painting. . . . Whether one becomes great is beside the point."

Geneva Handy Southall (1975), is a concert pianist and musicologist who was professor of Afro-American and African Studies from 1970 to 1992. Southall worked for a decade to recover the music of Thomas Greene Wiggins, a blind former slave whose musical genius had long been treated only as a circus curiosity. "I found Blind Tom through the music," she said, "and when I first saw one of his scores, I knew that no 'idiot' wrote this music."

Rutherford Aris (1991), a native of England, is Regents' professor emeritus of chemical engineering and a student of calligraphy, Latin paleography, and ornithology as well as of science. In a university, he has said, "there should live on a sense of the unity of knowledge and of the juice and joy of its continual discovery and refreshment." His life, said a colleague, is "testimony to the sacredness and power of the imagination" and its ability to help us make connections.

Amy Magnusson, Class of 1911.

Phil Brain, Sr.,
alumnus and tennis
coach, about 1925.

BELOW:
Mark Yudoff,
fourteenth president
of the University of
Minnesota, with spouse
Judy Yudoff, 1997.

Ruby B. Pernell, faculty member in the
School of Social Work, 1954.

LEFT:
Sam Jacobson, member
of the Gopher men's
basketball team, during
the 1996–1997 season.

COMMON BONDS: A Memoir in Photographs of the UNIVERSITY OF MINNESOTA

ABOUT THE AUTHOR

archivist for the YMCA, a job she describes as the best in the world.

She edited a landmark reference tool, *Women's History Sources: A Guide to Archives and Manuscript Collections in the United States*, and is author of another Donning publication, *Proud Heritage: A History in Pictures of the YMCA in the United States*. She is past president and fellow of the Society of American Archivists.

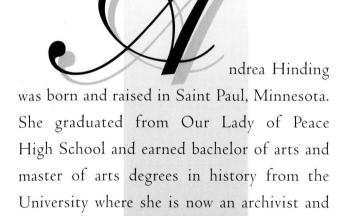

ndrea Hinding was born and raised in Saint Paul, Minnesota. She graduated from Our Lady of Peace High School and earned bachelor of arts and master of arts degrees in history from the University where she is now an archivist and faculty member.

Hinding joined the staff of the University Library in 1964 and is grateful to have worked since then in a world of books and manuscripts and ideas. In 1985 she became

A student on the Duluth campus, 1965.

A student at Duluth contemplates biochemistry in 1983.